Also by Frederick Seidel

PEACHES GOES IT ALONE

Peaches Goes It Alone

FREDERICK SEIDEL

FARRAR, STRAUS AND GIROUX
NEW YORK

Farrar, Straus and Giroux
175 Varick Street, New York 10014

Copyright © 2018 by Frederick Seidel
Printed in the United States of America
First edition, 2018

Library of Congress Cataloging-in-Publication Data
Names: Seidel, Frederick, 1936– author.
Title: Peaches goes it alone / Frederick Seidel.
Description: First edition. | New York : Farrar, Straus and
    Giroux, 2018.
Identifiers: LCCN 2018004948 | ISBN 9780374230531 (hardcover)
Classification: LCC PS3569.E5 A6 2018 | DDC 811/.54—dc23
LC record available at https://lccn.loc.gov/2018004948

Designed by Peter A. Andersen

Our books may be purchased in bulk for promotional,
educational, or business use. Please contact your local
bookseller or the Macmillan Corporate and Premium
Sales Department at 1-800-221-7945, extension 5442, or by
e-mail at MacmillanSpecialMarkets@macmillan.com.

www.fsgbooks.com
www.twitter.com/fsgbooks • www.facebook.com/fsgbooks

1   3   5   7   9   10   8   6   4   2

MITZ

CONTENTS

PEACHES GOES IT ALONE

ATHENA

Your favorites are the polar bears
Who these days have to walk on snot,
Global warming underfoot.
Snot, not snow, is now their natural habitat with climate change
And oceans rising.
The polar bears are doomed and ask you why.

The humid New York City that your arms are spread above
Like wings before you fly
To some new fantasy of yours of Mediterranean
Family happiness, which of course turns out to be
Passionately Greek tragedy pouring
Blue sky into dark clouds and it will storm.
The humid city opens up its heart
To yours.
What's needed is relief and a release
From.

Never mind your horrible claustrophobia
In the subway in from Astoria—
Never mind that there's Attic
Atavistic sibling rivalry at home—and a queen who's unkind.
Never mind.
And dad the king always off upstate hunting.

Greek America. These vulgar bejeweled peasants are kings and gods.

But what's with this heat wave! Are you in love?

Shudders of lightning and the smell of burning hair.
Electric magic in the sullen New York air.
Heat so intense even the cockroaches seek shelter.
This ultimate heat wave will abolish everything but air-conditioning
And evil and the fear of flying.

You're afraid of flying but you've made up your mind to fly.
You're afraid that all the passengers on the planet will die.
Your determination makes the Hudson River wink
As you rise wheels-up at long last to
Indomitable.

A sky of melting icebergs will rain down on Manhattan
When your plane lands safely back from Greece and your Greek cousins—
Back from Greek politics and debt and the unglued European Union.
The tires touch down on the New World tarmac and *squeal*
And all the plane applauds,
And your dreadful sister mocks,
Because you've almost overcome your fears . . .

The rain will bring relief to what
Your open arms are raised above, the way
The outstretched arms of Christ bless Rio,
Protect the poor and the police in the favelas,
Allow the Olympics to unspool its glories.

Hot rain is fatly splatting down
On Freedom Tower downtown.
Freedom Tower downtown goes up and up.
The hot hiss of hate turns to a hush.
Don't stop now, dearest, help us, don't stop.
The air is fresh. The rain has stopped.

Life isn't mostly Mozart,
But Mozart is a start, plays a part, as does all great art.

Late that night, in Lincoln Center's outdoor plaza,
After hours of tears, your heart burst into stars.

Your beautiful dark hair is not quite black, Athena.
Your beautiful smile is not quite meek, goddess.

Save us.

TOO MUCH

When even getting a haircut seems too much,
And trimming your toenails and fingernails takes too much strength,
When more than you have is what's required,
At least that's what you think,
And even the thought of reading a book makes you tired,
Then it's time to get on your motorcycle and ride far out to sea
And run out of money and blink S.O.S. and sink.

I was once in love myself.
I loved politics in those days as well.
Now I stare up at the sun.
I stretch out on the sidewalk under the moon
And greet each day as an adversary.
I thought I knew everything, then I met you.
It's rather like how a bald man once was hairy.

Everyone should be an optimist, of course.
Have the experience of marriage so you can have the experience of a divorce.
Sing, or rather scream, until you're hoarse.
Actually, you're acting like a baby.
You don't mean anything you're saying
When you're the middle of a volcano
And your lava starts to flow.

Actually, I'm screaming like a baby for a breast or the bottle,
Maybe a bottle of red, either Italian or French.

I'll get a haircut.
I'll cut my toenails. What's come over me?
I'm ready to fall in love with life.
I'm ready to drink her pee.
I'll take a shower after.

I'm ready to travel the world
Except I've already been.
Cape Coast Castle in Ghana
Is literally whitewashed white.
The building moans like a ghost under the enormous African sun.
The dungeon holding pen for slaves is a sacred place.
At the so-called Door of No Return, tourist African-Americans pose.

Triste Afrique!
Every single African head of state is corrupt.
Yesterday I was francophone and snowing, today I'm July.
I hear the whine of the mosquitoes.
They land on their oil rig of legs and drill down.
They're sort of our nurses
In the form of a proboscis of six hollow needles drawing blood.

I fell in love once and then it was over.
I found a long dark hair of hers long after.
I believe in the power of love to enslave.
Oxygen enters a vacuum of not and explodes.
Our slave ships unload us on the dock,
Prodrome of everything to come.
Too much is often enough. Too much is almost enough.

THE STORM

Lightning licks the salt off
The concrete of the sidewalk.
Flickering lightning
Shivers in the sky of July.

There's a storm coming
And, for a change, not just
From the White House.
Lightning sucks my eyes shut.

My hair stands on end when
(Not that I have much) you tell
Me there's more lightning
In the Congo than anywhere else in the world

Outside your arms.
That must be thunder
Rolling a hollow metal cylinder somewhere.
I should know. I'm from the Congo.

I should know
But don't know anything
In the heavily wet hot
New York Congo air.

La République démocratique du Congo,
Sometimes known as St. Louis, Missouri,
Is a land of love and lightning
Some of us come from.

I come from over yonder.
Listen to the thunder.
Can't we slip away to the moon
Unseen, in your submarine the *Congo Queen*?

Unhappiness will be destroyed once
The rain explodes.
Yes, but when—
And what till then?

I hear the elevator
Going *ding!* at each floor—
As required by law—as we go down,
To let the sight-impaired know where they are.

We embrace in the chandeliered marble lobby blindly.
The awning over the entrance is flapping.
The umbrella we open outside reverses
Itself in the blast.

THE EZRA POUND LOOK-ALIKE

It's always the same man
Who looks like Ezra Pound
Stretched out on the sidewalk
In front of Victoria's Secret.

No one knows what to make of his catastrophe.
What's it like to be Pound's look-alike?
Every day he pulls New York City
Over himself like a blanket and sleeps.

The sidewalk is a stairway to paradise
Down Broadway to the open road.
The possibilities ahead turn around and beckon.
A woman is marvelously shaking the tambourine.

Each slab of cement has its own story.
Don't step on the sidewalk cracks or do.
Everything is magical.
Things are about to happen.

The pitter-patter of a police helicopter overhead
Looking for you
In the streets below
Says it is beautiful but also it is true.

So when America is over,
What is there after?
There's more America, comerado!
There's always more.

Canoeing in northern Canada
Where wolves howl in the night,
And then rain tries to tear your tent apart,
Is just the same as Manhattan.

How sweet when you're American
To hear how grown-up you are
From the lady tousling your hair
Who can't see into your brain.

She might as well be a high-rise in the clouds
Reaching down to pat your curls.
Your face is at the level of her thing
And will be for the rest of your life.

You're where babies come out
And you are young forever,
And grow up
Only so far.

You're green as a grasshopper, America,
And jump that high.
You were green as a salad recently,
Which means summer is ending.

The future isn't over,
Even for the people left out.
It used to be there was no place that wasn't
Your stepmother making you a pie.

I RIDE AN OLD PAINT

My silly body fell down a set of stairs.
My big body doesn't always know who I am.
Doesn't recognize who it's with or how or why.
My silly body isn't always my buddy.
It doesn't always know where it is.
It fell down a flight of stairs.

It doesn't always know who's the boss.
It's like having your horse shot out from under you
While you're on your way to compete at the rodeo.
Are you the boss or the horse?
Life is always on the way to the rodeo
And suddenly your horse, Old Paint, ain't
Under you no more, cowboy, and you're on a gurney
At Greenport Hospital on your way to being X-rayed,
A hospital famous for its incompetence
But also for how pleasant the emergency room staff is.

Your body is a bag of love you walk around in.
My body turned the wrong way and stepped into thin air.
It could have died, with me on top of it in the crew compartment.
I'm in the cockpit on top of the rocket.
I can see a smudge of darkness in the distance
Which is a thunderstorm out over Long Island Sound.

I am alone with myself in my helmet of bone,
Checking for messages on my iPhone.
Now I will go back to going from here to there.
Wish me a safe journey with a nodule on one lung
Discovered in the X-ray after my body fell down.

Reader, I am the words that you are reading.
Reader, when I have long since ceased to exist,
I will be looking at you while you read this.

I am the enormous, extreme
Smile of summer rain.

MISS CHARLOTTE

Bring back the all-girls boarding schools for pedigreed girls
Where, morning and night, girls dressed and undressed.
Luxurious lawns and trees rode to hounds.
Horses the girls owned waited in padded stalls.

Think of the cold showers these aristocrats took.
Think of the dorm-room mirrors which sometimes saw
A cold girl lying on top of a warm girl
While a pretty girl with a pimply face on her bed on her back watched.

Have two rules, Miss Charlotte said:
Hard, good work and much fun.
She was addressing two favorites, Grits and little Bun-Bun.
There was gymkhana and dressage and raising the flag and French.

Keep up with the times, Miss Charlotte said. *Don't be narrow.*
Pile up on traditions and remember,
With God all things are possible.
On, on, with Foxcroft. Dare not let her die.

These ball gowns were tomboys who curtsy and bow.
These tigers were geldings life milks like a cow.
In life's cotillion, girls had to learn how
To be kapos at Dachau.

Kapos at Dachau, kapos at Dachau,
And pigeon-shooting on horseback at their plantations.
Once upon a time, Du Pont, Mellon, Frick, Whitney, Astor . . .
Astor was a disaster.

What got into Bun-Bun Astor
To make Miss Charlotte, who loved her, walk right past her?
Each child learned how to be her horse's master
And complete the dressage routine a little faster.

Night softly turns into light.
The gun Bun-Bun lifts out of her bra
Fires, blinding the room, flashing delight, killing Miss Charlotte outright.
Now the sun is fully up hurrah.

Miss Charlotte thought she heard a scream,
And woke from her dream.
Then began to weep.
Then went back to sleep.

MODIGLIANI

Masturbating in front of women who work for you or want to,
Women who have plenty to gain or lose in this,
Seems to be a new thing men in power do.
It's as big as the White House
When they pull it out.
They think they're performing
On a nine-foot concert grand piano.

The genius leading this country believes he's the Christ child.
The weather in his head is not mild.
He keeps tweeting and playing golf and getting riled.
It was the winter wild.
Constitutional democracy was defiled.
The poor and disadvantaged were reviled.
He wants the poor and disadvantaged who aren't white exiled.

The emperor Heliogabalus occupies the White House
In the fairy tale until he gets impeached
And daylight savings time and spring come back.
President Elagabalus of the United States
(And his unspeakably disgusting life)
Abandoned himself to the grossest pleasures and ungoverned fury.
It's getting dark early.

Each time the sun goes down,
One knows it will never rise again.
That's when your father is eaten by a shark
And your mother is raped in Central Park.
And you hear the sweet song of the meadowlark.
It was in the Three Arts Bookshop on Delmar Boulevard in St. Louis
That I first saw a Skira book of Modigliani nudes with pubic hair.

The crumbling New York subway system declares the glory of God.
The platforms fill with the homeless fleeing the terrible cold.
The very next day a soft breeze turns Manhattan into Key West
With bikini sunlight and birds singing.
The H3N2 virus drills up the streets,
Jackhammers of fevered, sobbing coughing.
The flu vaccine this year is hilariously only ten percent effective.

In this most bitter winter, there you were, Amalia, who can't carry a tune,
Singing away sublimely at the Metropolitan Opera in my dream,
An enormous voice under the lights, and then I saw
A stagehand carrying a painted stage prop of the moon, your insignia,
Aloft on a stick across the stage to indicate divinity.
The beauty of the voice is blinding.
The operatic moonlight is anoxic.

A hooded cobra rises center stage, swaying, in a trance, to kiss
Amalia Karabas, goddess of the moon,
Who teaches gifted high school kids in Queens.
So hopelessly endowed with charm she is,
Plus the Greek music magic of her name,
Kids and cobras go into a trance and dance.
She's why her students are so markedly advanced.

I was a Traveller then upon the moor,
Not getting very far.
It was my sunset voyage to the moon.
Illegals like myself still try to get there.
Maybe the Russians think it's fine
To watch the West decline,
But not my goddess fresh from Ancient Greece.

There's a Modigliani show on right now at the Tate Modern in London,
And the nudes have been hung in one room so we can stare.
And you'll come with me if you care, and we'll stare if we dare.
Outside, the Thames flows swiftly past, indifferently,
Not having heard of Modigliani.
Not having heard of the *London Review of Books*.
And the art critics, who are a bunch of crooks.

And lovely Billy Rayner died the other day,
Who lived a contemporary life but as if in another era,
Who was an extreme expression of graceful kindness,
With an upper-class almost-lisp that was a kind of classic
With which he joyfully traveled the world, painting and marveling,
With humor and sweetness, and now he is gone.
The man was a gentleman and was entirely someone.

And young Glykeria Papathanasiou,
Whose name gives you something extra to do,
Was always intending to return to her town in Greece,
Once she got her New York City accounting degree, to give Greece a try.
She saw the president of the United States attacking the FBI, and lie.
She saw Los Angeles hillsides of houses on fire,
And Houston underwater, and heard the global town crier.

Two things we can expect to see, Mary-Kay.
The old bent over their walkers.
The young talking on their smartphones.
Neither one is you or me.
This is no longer a country.
This is a country of the crippled and elderly
And the young who will eventually be.

AND NOW GOOD-MORROW TO
OUR WAKING SOULS

I wake each morning
To the sound of awful coughing
Coming from the street
Six floors below.
The same man sits there,
Wide awake at dawn,
On a narrow ledge, low to the sidewalk,
Barely wide enough
Not to cough and fall off.
The store he's outside is a Petco,
Closed of course at this hour,
Food and treats and toys for pets,
Leashes and collars
And bondage for dogs.
I wake early.
I let the light wake me.
I leave the bedroom curtains open
To have the light in the room.
From the bed, still in bed,
I listen to the coughing.
I walk over to the window.
The window is open
With the air conditioner on.
Time to be someone.

Time to put clothes on.
What have you done?
What will you do?
What will I do—what have I done!

IN LATE DECEMBER

FOR MITZI ANGEL

The man using the pay phone on Wall Street,
His back to you, is using it as a urinal,
And urinating—only logical!
Our degradation is complete.

The young woman, a crazy smile pickled in brine,
Cross-legged on the sidewalk in a T-shirt that says TOMORROW,
Holds a sign telling her sad story.
She's reading a paperback of *Lolita*, stealthily, behind the sign.

She could be you—
Stranger things have turned out to be true.
He could be me—
Don't rule out the possibility.

This shirtsleeves Christmas weather is lovely
And seriously weird.
El Niño is how Jesus was—
Both changed the climate.

Everyone will have a home. Everyone
Is safe and warm.
The homeless sleep on a bed of roses and sip ice wine (German *Eiswein*).
They spend their time deciding where they want to dine.

They spend the rest of their time thinking about the sublime
And exhuming corpses
So they don't have to beg for a living
From the living.

They bring back billions of bodies
And pile them in the apartment building lobbies
And repopulate the financial world with the dead
Like a dog bringing back a stick.

The stick is what was underground
Back in sunlight.
Cadavers and cremains hump on walkers down Wall Street
And a homeless hand reaches out to them for baksheesh.

She could be you!
Stranger things have turned out to be true.
He could be me—
I don't discount the possibility.

Jews, Christians, Muslims, others—it's Christmas morn.
Aloha, *amici*, Christ is born!
Flowers are fooled into thinking it's spring.
The little city birds sing.

ENGLAND NOW

FOR PAUL KEEGAN

I like to be dead.
That's what the dead say.

I'd rather be dead than so-called alive.
I like the lack of feeling.

But you know what?
That's the way I've always felt.

That's my way.
I'm feeling good.

I haven't been big on feeling.
I haven't been alive that much.

It rains all the time and it's cold in July.
Somewhere down south,

In the tropical humidity and heat
Of my brain below the belt,

Is where I vote.
I don't want any.

I eat what's there.
I don't import.

I am England
Under these newish circumstances.

A people who are proud to be dead said
So loud and clear.

AMSTERDAM

In Amsterdam, you order women à la carte
From glassed-in boxes where they pose—as at an Automat or Horn & Hardart—
And when you indicate the one you choose,
She lets you in the box and you take off your shoes.

I'm noticing my legs in Amsterdam—which look so old!
Dear legs in Amsterdam—no good, not looking good!
I'd make you better-looking if I could.
The foot they end in also isn't great.

In summertime in Amsterdam it's herring time—
You throw your head back and open wide.
I took the Trans Europ Express from Paris up, in the sublime
Of being young and ravishing and magnified

By going fast first-class, bringing galleys of our magazine, The Paris Review,
To our Dutch printer, with our latest issue's interview—
Back in '61, when the CIA thought art helped and when the West had
        not yet won,
But almost had, and when my young legs and feet were fun.

Oh my, my feet look odd, as if they're on the verge of speech,
As if they want to sing a song
By a canal, about they won't be here for long.
I won't be here for long, they sing, singing each to each.

The next line of the song is: I don't think art helps much.
Or maybe as a crutch.
But the overwhelming Rembrandts in the Rijksmuseum start
A little nosebleed in my heart.

PARIS

I wear a suicide belt I detonate
And make my City of Light
A coprophagic tomb.
This is the End of Days.
This is what we've been waiting for always.
I walked over to the Hudson River, heading for Mars.
Each poem of mine is a suicide belt.
I say that to my girlfriend, Life.

Welcome to paradise, and goodbye.
Stay away, stay home, don't gather in numbers.
Of course we want to assemble to demonstrate
I wasn't born to fear all this,
But every one of you will receive a lei,
And martyrs will receive a lei and a virgin.
Oh yes it's showtime and yes apocalypse.
It's bombed-to-bits applause-applause

Gouging out the ice cream with a scoop
To eat some soft,
And then comes Creutzfeldt-Jakob disease,
Also known as love.
You eat the other person's brain,
Which makes her you.
You cut her head off
And scoop out the fresh.

I walked across the park.
Yo, Central Park!
Another time,
I sat on a park bench in Stockholm
And talked to New York.
I used to make a pilgrimage
To the funny stunted statue of Pierre Mendès-France
In the Luxembourg Gardens,

But suddenly I was upended,
Things went almost upside down.
I was walking down the street.
I walked around downtown.
It was fall, but before the leaves fell
I was gouging my brain out with a scoop,
Or do I mean gouging my heart out?
She would say what heart.

I wear a suicide belt that every day I detonate.
I say that to my girlfriend, Life.
Each poem of mine is a suicide belt
And I explode into a pink pâté sticking to the street.
It's time to go to London on the Eurostar
And blow up underneath the Channel.
Schoolchildren with me on the train
Want to hear Big Ben.

When I'm in London,
I walk on stilts, up high, from Claridge's
To Mount Street Gardens, and breathe.
The birds are singing.
Across the street is Purdey's and their shotguns
To kill birds with beautifully.
The streets everywhere are bipolar
And wear a suicide belt.

They wear a suicide vest.
Mendès-France got the French out of Indo-China.
Who will get the suicide bombers out of Paris?
Françaises, Français, aidez-moi!
You catch sight of yourself in the mirror and my God
There's a big booger hanging out of your nose
That's obviously been there all along
While you were busy being Gallic and charming.

Who spread the rumor Paris was fun?
Who had such fantasy?
Who never knew Paris minus you?
Who said gay Paree?
Cole Porter's Paris, pearl of the Occident,
Didn't plan to be bombed like this.
Paris will resist and Paris to exist
Will bomb those fervent little shits to fervent little bits.

BAUDELAIRE IN BRUSSELS

Some people say sex is like riding a rainbow.
Maybe theirs is.
I say I fall on a grenade each time.
My rainbow-on-a-runway took off practically
Straight up from the infirmary
To reach the thermosphere,
And blew up above Brussels, Paris, etc.—
And here's the nurse. *Nurse!*
I had a stroke.
I had another stroke.
I can't lift my prepuce head from the bed.
Someone said my poison poems
Are flowers someone brought into the room,
Flowers that leave behind a sonic boom.

TRUMP

I look past the big face of my computer
At what was once New York
Outside my window
And now is a plateau
Of smiling bra-less
Breasts of the contestants.
It's time to wake
From this cryogenic sleep
In which I've been preserved, and vote.

The endlessness of America ends.
And what an ending.
A second-stage booster rocket ascending
From the one below that's downward-trending.
Enough protein to get you there—
But not beyond—
Required rebirth
Into another form of life.
Namely, Donald Trump.

I turn the TV off
Which comes back on
All on its own.
It's all about climate change
And fracking girls.
And every bidet is transgender

Or ought to be.
Trans is the time of day.
Many people these days are Trump or trans or gay.

On Emotion Avenue in Queens—
Near Trouble Street—
Cops on horseback clatter
In their yellow slickers
Through the springtime drizzle
Toward Black Lives Matter.
White working-class
Clouds of tear gas
Cloud Emotion.

TRUMP FOR PRESIDENT!

A perfect week for digging up the block.
If you care, you repair
The infrastructure or it will despair.
Bear with the noise! We aren't made of air.
Tyrannosaurus rex on tires, gorging horribly,
Fucks the street in bursts and jerks.
The operator riding it bucks and charges forward
And resumes his hippopotamus mouthfuls.

The scene's a slaughterhouse
With dead meat screaming.
Maybe the concrete is fully conscious?
Major surgery without anesthesia.
You'll need earplugs and a hardhat
While this berserk year runs amok.
We actually need to talk.
What now? Now what?

We are poor little lambs who have lost our way.
We are little black sheep who have gone astray.
O say can you see what we're about to be?
What am I, chopped liver?
O say can you see
We're about to be
The Nuremberg Rally
In an alley?

I text the sky—hi, sky!—
O infinite and blue!
In a green pasture up in the blue sky a cow chews her heavenly cud,
A garland of orchids around her neck.
Cow-eyed Hera—goddess!—but not goodness—
Not calm, patient, selfless abundance—
Not Hindu! Not moo-cow moo!
But, Donald darling, unmistakably you.

GENERALISSIMO FRANCISCO FRANCO
IS STILL DEAD

Every time I sleep I leave a stain.
When I wake up, I climb out of a drain
And step into my feet and it is plain
That when I walk away I leave a lane
Of garbage on the carpet in the train.

Francisco Franco (El Caudillo) pokes his head up from the drain
Where he's been hiding with Saddam Hussein.
He waterboards the peasants with champagne.
Now maybe they'll vote to give this madly inane
Hitler buffoon his very own nuclear codes, let democracy reign!

Make Spain great again! I shouldn't touch it but I can't refrain
And don't restrain
Myself so what was once a tiny grain
Of pain
Is now a roaring lion with a mane.

Franco needs water for his golf courses so we can't complain
Out loud but it's insane—insane
Monsoons of rain
Drowning the automatic sprinkler systems that maintain
The greens, blinding windshields worldwide, Spain to Maine.

I can't stop rhyming! I can't. It's my domain!
Making more or less musical noise out of my fascist disdain.
I choose Francisco Franco, weakling strong man of Spain,
As my alter ego, bearer of my terror over what I can't attain
In the few years I have left, the minutes that remain . . .

Lacking tenderness, not something you can go to the store and obtain,
But which anyway does not pertain
To piloting an airplane
Dropping bombs on innocent civilians who remain
In pieces in the street under the boiling sun, Spaniards, pieces of Spain.

Don't drink and drive. Don't text while driving. Don't kill Lorca. Maintain
The good health of your car and tires and don't explain
To anyone when you're in the red-light district but remain
Alert also on the subway and don't feign
Ignorance because, though Franco is still dead, long may Franco reign!

ABUSERS

Every woman who wants to be spanked should be
Spanked for wanting to be.
It's for excitement and as punishment for her ascent.
She should be put on a pedestal so you can look up to her

From below and get outstanding news and views
From beneath and see what you want to see.
Look at her clean machine, her beautiful guillotine!
Erect as a hooded cobra about to strike, exactly what a hissing vagina looks like!

They've made a list of those of us not necessarily as innocent as just
Taking an attractive young subordinate to a nice publisher's lunch.
I mean, the intern in her allegation reported me
For fancy perverse intercourse coerced, which got my name listed in blood-red.

I'm a sexist sexting and swagger down Broadway and end up in mayhem.
How many women can you butt-dial in one evening!
I'm interested only in the power of their flesh.
I turn the fire hose on them when they protest.

Sexual harassment and sexual abuse and also incest,
All of them, of course, utterly commonplace,
Are suddenly being exposed under our narcissistic, misogynist, male chauvinist
Chief of state with orange hair, how odd, releasing revolution.

There's no romance to the violence—and no one is innocent—
And it's incurable.
The women of the world are almost driven mad.
And they become a firing squad.

The little girl whose father invaded her
Became a woman who could not outgun
The little girl inside her who's her father's wife.
Kill, kill, kill your father with your ruined life.

The girl with the father still inside her has to lead.
Victims will turn to her to find the road.
The crowd of millions of women is rhythmically chanting *Make them pay!*
The cops are breaking down the door with a search warrant.

Bring back that old-time Hollywood studio head—bring us his head!
His brutal bulk greenlights the groaning casting couch.
The crowd roar is women victims who have filled a worldwide stadium to see
The male presidents of all their countries beheaded.

Meanwhile, one glorious woman in London grows an ever larger, greater soul.
Her shyness displays a winged magnificence.
Watch a fine flame flare.
Watch a flower impersonate Robespierre.

Saudi women will get the right to drive
Because it's time. Because the sun is in the sky.
The world is nearing war.
The homeless clog the streets.

NOVEMBER 9, 2016

I can't hear you if in fact you're speaking.
It's like I'm dead, or else you are.
Or else I'm out of juice—
My cell phone's dead again.
God bless your lovely face I can't see!

I'll use a cleaver to cut my hair.
I'll wear asparagus for underwear.
I took the elevator to the thirteenth floor
To find the fiends.
They opened the door.

Of course I know years later I'll still feel afflicted
With the thought of having once.
Years later, still feel remorse, regret,
Wide as the mighty Mississippi,
For what we did, and yet

I vividly remember: *Here we go over the edge!*
Niagara Falls. Wheeee.
Heavenly to vote, leaping off a window ledge!
My country, 'twas of thee.
Sweet land of one, two, three

JUMP

Into the swamp, below the buttocks crack squatting over the dump.
Caw-caw crows circling in the sky above their cause.
Roll credits. Voiceover of vultures.
Caw-caw-caw American applause.

I can't hear you but we're still speaking.
I can't see you either, if you're there.
It's like I'm dead, or you are.
Or else I'm out of juice again.
God bless your beautiful, your spacious, skies!

We don't know the answer to
Outside New York City what's happened to
Because he lives midtown
In a tower of global-warming gold.
The traffic situation midtown is possibly the end of the world.

A DIP IN DAVID SALLE'S POOL

This is a different sort of space race.
To the stars through adversity!
A right hook to the jaw and the planet sees stars!
I'm doing laps in a pool to escape Earth's gravity
And liftoff from world poverty and climate calamity.
From East Hampton to the stars!
To the stars through prosperity!
The pledge of art is to lift.

Liftoff from world poverty.
Liftoff from climate calamity.
Liftoff from the insanity.
Liftoff from my own inanity.
Life crawled out of a warm ocean, oozed out of the ooze,
Into the Parthenon.
Every person alive has his/her/their very own first name.
But when the Earth ends no one will read this poem.

I think about the folks back home several million miles away.
I feel quite dizzy thinking.
I feel I'm
Far away.
I watch the dark go by.
I left the solar system, looking forward to
Another system.
I saw an eye not looking at me.

Spacetime spangles starry spaghetti on the pool's surface.
Space is what it comes to.
Space is what you live through.
The galaxies are what is left.
Everything is different.
I'd never met a woman who didn't drive a car.
I thought, that's just not who they are.
I'd never known one who didn't know how to.

Women fight in the army now.
Their change of costume changes the world.
Women have changed into themselves.
Women do everything and one will be president.
Consommé of Comets.
Roasted Breast of Nearby Stars.
Black Hole Pie. Brandy and Cigars.
Menu for our colony on Mars.

On Sunset Beach on Shelter Island,
Time magnified my dying hand
Into so many grains of sand.
In this saltwater lap pool behind this splendid house,
Time floats into new spaces in space.
The pool-length slot of water without a ladder to get in
Reflects the bird-soaked sky—and once I'm in,
I space-walk tethered to the eighty-year-old man swimming.

DUCATI YEARS, DUCATI DAYS

I had a girlfriend who dumped me for a better job—
Which, frankly, made me laugh so hard I started to sob.

I'd been so disgustingly highfalutin—so grand!—ballooning on hot air
Above green pincushion fields with trees stuck in down there,

Snootily floating above and looking down,
My drinker's red nose tilted up arrogantly, red-nosed circus clown

Floating above life's road-rage-in-a-maze.
Ah, those were lovely Ducati years and Ducati days!

I rode my racers and felt superior.
Nothing could catch me—nothing inside me—just an exterior.

Almost all Ducati motorcycles in those fine days were red.
We Ducatisti rode red-hot Italian beauties on the track and in bed.

I squeeze into my old red race-team jacket to remember.
Rosso di competizione . . . but it's freezing December

Out on the street as I walk off last night's alcohol, ballooned in bulging down.
I'm the Michelin Man-Made-of-Tires, a clown

In down, tethered unsteadily to the ground,
With not too many more laps left to wobble around.

Skewered me like a kebab.
Left me for a better job.

CHERNOBYL

Each of us is also a ghost.
Most you can see.
They look like the person you are.
Hers is a series of beautiful blurred action
Images of an antelope attacking and killing
And eating a fully grown alpha lion.
The lion's broken head
Sticks out of his mane on the pillow, bloody-red, almost dead,
And then the reactor exploded, typical of love.

Hello, hello, hello, hello.
I'm here, it's me, hello. I'm my ghost.
I'm the heavenly piercing freshness of no pain after your pain.
I'm the soft perfume of warm August rain.
I'm the rope of distance that ties me to you
That makes no sense, but I do, and it does.
I want to be huge,
And a deluge, and a refuge.
I want to be your forever voice message.

I want to be late dinners at the outdoor restaurant
In the sweet radioactive night air
Under platinum stars and the sky
In the tiny town square,
And the restaurant's little string of electric lights
Lighting those nights

The year the Chernobyl disaster kept the tourists away,
And Alzan the dog stayed back at the house
We rented, my dream dog, a dog like a song.

One goes on living and wonderful things
Go on going wrong,
But something else wonderful comes along.
Chernobyl meant don't eat dairy
For fear the cows were eating radioactivity,
So we ate anyway and thrived.
The Crillon in Paris had a no-dogs policy
But not that Chernobyl summer
Because—no customers, no one there!

If you're not unlucky, life is long
And something wonderful will come along.
Thirty-one years have passed since 1986.
I'm remembering my dog.
I recollect the radioactive steam of love.
Our present political disaster is vaster and expanding faster,
But I do. We do. Two ghosts kiss.
Leave me a voice message
And say you are.

EPITHALAMION
FOR STEIN AND STEIN

Two hummingbirds visit the privet,
Flickering your eyes, drumming your heart,
Here and gone before you blink.
You walk airborne toward the start.

Fifteen minutes' drive to the beach and ocean,
Ten to Long Beach and the bay.
Jimmy the dog is asleep in a flower bed.
The sprinklers mist a rainbow in the Garden of Eden.

It's the hiss of the hose in the heat
Hosing down the sidewalk, fresh and neat,
And releasing the delicious odor of hot concrete.
It's dripping out of a swimming pool onto hot-under-your-feet.

You're a minute away from Main Street
And minutes away from the vulgar, sweet,
Tiny downtown, no bigger than a Twitter tweet,
And the American Hotel porch where you'll eat.

THREE POEMS THAT MENTION
PIERRE LEVAL
AND ONE THAT DOESN'T

I

We're Getting There

A newborn fading in an old photograph now lost
Is the one picture of Geraldine, my maternity nurse—
If Geraldine is what her name was—but the photograph is lost.
Newborn goes to college, which is freedom and strange.
You do things.
You do other things.
You sort of know what you're doing.
You go off course to stay true.
Girls are not everything but they're everything.
Cambridge, Harvard, *Hahvud*, Paris, London, Pound, Eliot.

You grow up more or less happily and unhappily
In an Eton collar and little-boy
Short pants, plus itchy gray flannel knickers and corduroy knickers
With knee-high wool stockings,
Sometimes with a tartan pattern,
That are always falling down.
Try to wear long pants that you're not entitled to
Before Class Six and they'll be stripped

Off you by upperclassmen in the all-white, all-boys, Episcopalian school
And run up the flagpole, is the rumor!

Black in a white uniform stands next to a baby carriage
Holding a white dot just born.
The family will move to a bigger place in the Senate Apartments
Next door to the Congress Hotel,
Buildings that are on Union Boulevard, remembering the Civil War.
There is a photograph, now lost, taken during
The first few weeks of a life, showing a black maternity nurse
Who would have been called "colored" eighty years ago.
Eighty years later, newborn bops down Broadway on his way to see his friend
Leval, full of jazz, full of glad, and lives forever.

II
The Vision

My dear pal is Judge Pierre Leval,
And a just judge is he—
And the national authority on copyright fair use, additionally!
The United States Court of Appeals for the Second Circuit
In downtown Manhattan is where he presides,
And where he sits and judges in his formidable robes, but one fine day
He was transported in a vision
To the innocent sounds of a more just world
And the long-ago high-pitched voices he'd gone to summer camp with,
And the joy and the freshness
Was so vivid he could only stare—he was there!

III

The Staircase

FOR JONATHAN GALASSI AND TENOCH ESPARZA

A man strutting down Park Avenue in front of me trips
And glares down at the sidewalk as if the sidewalk were at fault.
I fell down a staircase of stairs in the middle of the night
Without assigning blame to the stairs or to myself.

The fellow who tripped is beautifully dressed.
How did he vote in the last presidential election, I want to know.
I don't know why I think of Inverness in Scotland
And the marvelous trip Pierre Leval and I took to the whisky Highlands

With bicycles we brought along but never rode—
My fault—once I discovered how many hills there were,
And after my harrowing ride to Culloden Moor.
Skye blinded me, as later in my life Bali would, and still later, Tahiti.

I trip but I don't fall! is my motto,
Even when I'm falling down a flight of stairs.

IV

Self-Portrait with a Stranger in the Mirror

Ever know somebody who simply doesn't seem to age,
Who instead of showing signs of decrepitude stays young,

Whose skin without a facelift stays
Eerily smooth as honey,
As if the skin itself were
Some kind of marvelous, beautiful monster
That talks like somebody young and walks like somebody young
And orders the usual
Pastrami salmon on a buttered, toasted bialy
At Barney Greengrass, and in the men's room mirror sees
Fangs covered by mold
And a man totally old.

THANKSGIVING 2016

The girl with the face
As charming as her voice
Has a beautiful ass
Filling out her tan pants.

Depression doesn't stand a chance
Confronted with this one!
What planet are you on
In your beret, singing?

We are giving thanks,
All eyes on you.
We're alive.
We're living.

We listen to you singing
Reasons for being.

TO MAC GRISWOLD

Suddenly I'm ready to eat the world,
Starting with the food on my plate.
The waiter asks if everything's all right.
Everything's great.
Everything looks the same but nothingness is night.
Time to go back upstairs into more electric light.

My jaunty step is oral, enjoying everything.
This election year is the beginning.
The national falling apart will amount to something.
Suddenly I'm able to walk outside.
Suddenly I'm able to walk away.
Rain is falling on the other side of the street.

Thank you for the delicious food.
Thank you for my delicious mood.
It's time to get back upstairs and smirk and shirk work.
Writing poems is like being in Sing Sing singing.
It's like being a prisoner of what you want to do
And being imprisoned for being a prisoner.

What makes a poet bird sing in Sing Sing,
Beak ready to say absolutely anything?
The cage and the rage
And a future of old age
Make a squealer sing in Sing Sing.
That's what this admirer of yours is made of.

What surpasses being in love, unless it's love?
What's better than gardens and landscape?
Who described gardening as "the slowest of the performing arts"?
Who wrote about green grandeur?
Who rode to hounds over timber fences?
Who got thrown out of Foxcroft?

Dearest Grits, my beautiful powerhouse ex,
You goaded me into the happiness you guided me through.
Just saw Marco Island, Florida, on a map.
Remember the Christmas lights, the beach?
The Parthenon, the pink coat, the picnic
With Alzan in the olive grove,

Barbados, Ghana, the Hôtel Raphael, the Hôtel Lenox,
Les Gourcuff, snowy Sag Harbor,
Motorcycles in summer Sag Harbor.
Well, I don't often think back,
But right now I do. Mac, I too do,
By the light cast by you.

MOTHER'S DAY NIGHT

Maurizio Pollini stays in his room at the Carlyle Hotel
Practicing endlessly on a baby grand for his coming concert
At Carnegie Hall.
My friend Dino Zevi's room as it happens is one floor below.

Dino Zevi rests in his room at the Carlyle Hotel
Hearing the pleasant nearby faintly familiar piano voices
Of Chopin arriving from somewhere.
He leaves his room to take the elevator.

It is the week of the big art auctions in New York
And Dino Zevi, who has come over from London
For them, leaves his room to do
What he's here for, trailing an invisible airborne ribbon of Chopin.

The elevator door opens and inside along with the attendant
Is Maurizio Pollini. Good morning.
I've been listening with pleasure to you playing Chopin.
Oh dear, I am so terribly sorry if I am bothering you.

This happens morning after morning
In the elevator. Good morning.
I am so terribly sorry if I am disturbing you
With my playing.

The weather in New York at last is really warm.
Ninety-two degrees Fahrenheit or thirty-three degrees Celsius.
I would remind you that Zevi is married to one
Of the loveliest women in the world, Anne-Laure, who isn't here.

Pollini, some time ago, slipped and fell and injured his spine.
He walks stooped over but never mind.
The Carlyle is a place of harmonious dissonance. Pollini sort of floats.
It is a place of ruthless romance, if you ever get a chance.

The world is a place of harmony, if you ever get a chance.
At the auction last night, a 1982 painting by Basquiat, who died so young,
Sold for 110.5 million, unbelievable
And altogether too believable.

It is like the hysteria of goodwill on Mother's Day night
In the happy crowded restaurants of Manhattan.
I salute my friend Zevi as the elevator of art ascends ecstatically
On wings of money and art.

Of course, even if you are Pollini you must practice endlessly.
Even if you slip your disc you must persist and insist.
Even after your death, the beauty is in the most delicately enforced gestures
Of your wrist.

NEAR THE NEW WHITNEY

In the Meatpacking District,
Not far from the new Whitney,
In a charming restaurant,
I showed how charming I can be.
I showed how blue my eyes can be.
I showed I can be Dante first catching sight of Beatrice.

The maître d' was new to me.
The sudden sight of her, so gently lovely,
Threw me at the pressed-tin ceiling, where I stuck.
I asked her where I was, her name was Emily.
I don't know who the ceiling was.
I doubt pressed tin was what it was.

I was moonstruck.
Now I could only look up.
American art used to be risky.
American art used to be frisky
And drink a lot of whisky.
I looked up at Emily, not far from the new Whitney.

Seventy years ago,
There were violently drunkard painters downtown who,
Many of them, painted violently
In the Hamptons also.
Now they were in the splendid new Whitney, dead
Instead.

I wished I had a sled dog's beautiful eyes,
One blue, one brown,
To mush across the blizzard whiteout
Of sexy chirping chicks and well-trimmed
Bearded white young men.
You see how blue my old eyes aren't.

I drank an after-dinner tumbler of whisky
Not far from the new Whitney,
A present from the maître d'.
Sweet Lagavulin single malt filled me with infinity
Sixteen years old, while the girl
Smiled softly.

ROUPELL STREET

I was walking down Roupell Street,
Avoiding all the drunks.
I live in a little house
In little Roupell Street
Where I find it hard to sleep.

I live in a little gray house
The size of a little gray mouse.
I tell my good friend Maya
Who lives a street away
I'd rather put up with the noise in New York and live on Broadway.

They come out of pubs nearby.
They wobble over from Waterloo.
They wake me up in the middle of the night,
Bawling their boozy goo.
I call the police when they scream and fight—

But only if there's blood!
Come visit me, I'll cook you dinner.
I just don't advise you to stay over!
I love little Roupell Street because it's sweet,
But you see what I mean.

I'm Mitzi Angel of Faber & Faber,
I live on *You Smell* Street—
Rhymes with *Roupell* Street.
I love my street because it's sweet
As strawberries and cream, but you see what I mean!

(Some people say Roople *to rhyme with* Scruple.*)*

HALL OF FAMER

I magically became Stan Musial
When I was a little boy
Every time I stood at home plate,
Too young to wear spikes.

I was the St. Louis Cardinals' Hall of Famer
Stan the Man
Every time I grabbed
My three-quarter size big-league bat

And twisted myself around
To face the pitcher with my back,
And cocked the bat high in the air behind my Cardinals cap
In Musial's famous corkscrew batting stance.

I stared back at the pitcher over my shoulder,
Waiting for the future,
Ready to rip a fastball
Out of Sportsman's Park.

I was in heaven, age eleven, nineteen forty-seven,
Already playing hardball
In Teddy Simmons's
Westmoreland Place backyard.

Put some mustard on it, Teddy, and throw hard
Until our syrupy summer evening sun goes down.
I hate to see that evening sun go down.
I'm protecting the strike zone and waiting for Ezra Pound.

AUTUMN

A man walks briskly away from his body
And from feeling slightly sick on a blazingly fall day.
The sky is fresh perfection, without a cloud of illness.
The air is clean and cool as a fountain.
The heat of the last few weeks deflates.
The man walks as fast as he can up a mountain
In the middle of his head,
In the middle of a city.

Notwithstanding your attempts to indict me,
I will not fall ill, I refuse, he says.
He says, Some things are more delicious than other things,
Minister of doodle-y-doo,
Prince of sky after sky of blue.
Even in almost a drought,
Things can be succulent and full
And capable of merci beaucoup.

Sky after sky of blue, to match his eyes,
Is also the color he looks best in,
And also what these fall days have been so far, a fresh perfection.
A man should be wearing the sky.
A fellow should wear what he is walking under,
And when the day clouds over, especially so.
He's ready to travel via his smartphone to her gloriousness
Faster than the cars go in a Formula 1 race.

Behold his angel far away,
Who might as well be cocooned in outer space,
But in fact she's in a country where the sky is always gray,
And where the sky wants to stay that way.
If you make up your mind to,
You can be together in her weather.
Or if you'd rather,
And can't live without her, you can die.

Round head, round brain, jagged heart,
Your heart barnacled by too much . . .
A space traveler incapable of space travel,
Back from a failed mission,
Lands out at sea on the deck of a nuclear submarine
With armed warheads that has surfaced for this purpose.
It is a spectacular fall day, and the gorgeous air is dressed in blue,
And the worshiper turns to her neighbor and gives the kiss of peace.

The leaves will be falling soon to make things fresh and clean and new.
People walking their dogs bend down
To pick up after their dogs the dog doo,
People obeying a city ordinance they've finally got used to.
No one expected where they were heading.
They join hands at a worldwide wedding.
The police commissioner is there, the mayor.
On the steps, kilts are wailing bagpipes.

FOR X—WITH LOVE AND SQUALOR

My God, what a beautiful New York day!
If only getting old would go away!
Wings that used to lift me like a hawk
Before my dick turned into chalk
So I could pounce
On every girl and eat up every ounce
Is something I don't want to whine about.
I was walking down the street and I felt a sudden doubt.
I was circling in the sky
Looking down at potential prey and started to cry.

But what a beautiful day.
I take my usual constitutional down Broadway.
I walk faster than some.
I see a bearded Civil War veteran beating a drum.
People are looking at their cellphones and don't look.
Under the volcanoes, her terror writes a great book.
All the way away, she starts to cry
Under a moon in the daytime sky.
The giant with roaring wings she put a curse on has become
A hummingbird no bigger than her thumb.

QUAND VOUS SEREZ BIEN VIELLE

Fifty years from now you'll be my age
And old like me instead
Of young, and I'll be dead
And therefore won't be any good in bed,

But you won't either at that stage,
When your lunatic beauty will exist only on this page
From fifty years before, when it still could ravage
Me and turn a dainty Harvard man into a grunting savage

Who climbs a ladder through the stars to reach the moon,
And plucks at his laptop and it becomes a lute,
And writes an old man's poem of pursuit—
Earth rising to the moon to sing a saccharine tune

And leave below the geriatric horror of his appetite
And hide inside the moonlight high above the awful sight.

SHAKESPEARE

Every female animal is identical
For the mucho macho man with a small penis who slaughters
Mother Nature and her daughters.
Essentially no difference between Ophelia
And Cordelia.

No one with a brown or black skin is allowed
In. No one with a brown or black or yellow
Skin is allowed in the conservatory
Where the orchids are kept warm
And moist in His Majesty's mouth.

Every female animal is identical in that
They're all only a receptacle
To hold the king's seed, and out
Spring the flowers
Who later will get locked up in towers and

Armies are marching.
Shakespeare and his company of actors speak
The speech more or less
Outdoors in the green London rain under
Hardly any roof, and boys dressed up as girls.

Millions do. Dress up as girls.
A mass extinction of them took place every hour with
AIDS, as if the showerhead were sucking back the shower,
Taking back to heaven the cherished,
Perished water.

The lad playing Cleopatra droops and drops to the floor,
Instant express elevator right
Up to the top of Trump Tower.
Her words sprout wings of Shakespeare.
Things fall straight up

To heaven.
A mass extinction in the final act of the tragedy
Takes place all the time when
It's time and
It's time and

God the showerhead
Is unwatering
The flower bed.
The clouds inhale everything.
The gods inhale everything while bells across the nation ring,

Birds do sing,
Wherein I'll catch the conscience of the king,
Hey ding a ding, ding,
Sweet lovers love the spring,
And Hamlet tries to marry his mother.

WORST WHEN IT'S POETRY

Here's a naked fellow dressed up in some clothes,
Arrogantly flaunting what he actually loathes—
The Savile Row swagger and the nonchalant pose!
He's who he isn't and he makes sure it shows.

I'm Nobody! Who are you?
I'm thinking, what would Mother do?
And what would Kafka if he knew?
Emily Dickinson was Nobody, too!

I'd say the day looks like there's nothing new.
It's simply someone the sky is talking to.
Sprinklers on Central Park's Great Lawn are hissing mist,
A smell simply too delicious to exist.

Sweet, sweet, sweet! You drown in it, I've drowned.
The currents undersea wave our hearts around.
You'll be so happy that I'm cured of snoring and now I snore
No more.

There's an Emily I met downtown recently.
Dante's Beatrice suddenly appeared to me!
I don't know her last name.
Dante famously never was the same.

A maiden I don't know transfigured me
In one brief moment for eternity.
From one brief meeting with someone so young,
Dante was translated to a higher sphere and left our days of dung.

It's my opinion my friend Michael Hofmann is a wizard.
Every page of German, Hofmann eats a gizzard,
Translates the untranslatable
Words, words, words.

Worst when it's poetry—
But even Joseph Roth's *Radetzkymarsch*.
Mandelstam could absolutely not be—
Then Clarence Brown and Merwin came along and *did*.

I'm thinking green, but the English-speaking sky is blue.
I tell you what I'm going to do.
They tell me what they're going to do.
Here's what my words will do today.

The words are at the other end.
I'll have to drive.
I'll take the car.
It isn't far. That's where they are.

BARBARA EPSTEIN

Sometime near dawn, driving a stolen car
So fast I will never arrive,
Floating without a destination and without a license
Along the empty highways across the Mississippi from St. Louis,
Just the occasional big interstate truck's

Prong of headlights sticking into the dark
Through the misty summer odor of *to get away!*
At age fifteen, too young to drive or drink—
Is what I did a lot of, with a lot of drink,
And the driver's-side window open

To loll my head out to sniff the oncoming breeze like a dog,
Quaffing the opiate of the gigantic fields of Illinois,
Sucking in deep breaths of the husky
Thick bittersweet bituminous
Rising already at this early hour from the factory smokestacks

Of collapsing factories made of roseate bricks,
Ecstatic, as though of prednisone I had drunk,
And that cold black earth smell out in the boondocks.
And Vergil takes me by the hand as we descend
To meet the shades of Homer, Ovid, Horace, Lucan.

And I stop to give those greats a ride at dawn
And in their company at sunrise whoosh to wherever I belong
On wings of song.
How in the world does this connect to Barbara Epstein?
This is a way of bringing flowers to her shrine.

If I'm constantly stealing my father's cars, forever, she is forever
Founding co-editor of *The New York Review of Books*, and that's better—
Even though she nearly always canceled at the last minute
Every lunch date she ever made with anyone, or so it seemed!
One of the great editors

(And even in that wicked world everyone revered her)
Could be relied on to cancel
The lunch date with you she herself had made.
It was her *tic nerveux* to have to.
This is what happens when you think of someone no longer alive you love.

ENVOI

IN MEMORY OF JEANETTE BONNIER (1934–2016)

Someone dear to me
Rises from her hospice bed,
Removes her body and her hair,
Starts walking through the air transparently,
Starts walking through the air going somewhere.
Then I woke.

Birds singing ask if I believe in God.
The buds are budding on the trees.
Which seems so out of date to ask.
I don't but do.
I believe in you.
It's almost spring.

The planted center strip of Broadway
That tweets your voice, your face, your fate, starts to dawn.
I've been away.
They burst with buds.
In London and in Stockholm,
I survived.

And when God asks if you believe in God,
It's Stage IV pancreatic cancer asking.
A body asks if I believe.
In Stockholm, I do not.
The buds are budding on the trees on Broadway.
Birds are singing.

Thunder is my favorite color,
As are you. *Lightning.* But no more
Back and forth incessantly
On missions.
I just got back.
A hopeless mission.

Waded into an Asia
Of very deep morphine.
Kill death.
You can't until you die.
O death O death.
You can't kill death until you die.

I'd like to be a dove flying back and forth
Above the concrete fjord of Manhattan Island.
I bring green sprigs
Of nothing for a nest.
Sprigs of hope.
There is no hope.

Jeanette, the takeaway from this
Is spring is in effect
To no effect. Jeanette,
I don't believe
But do
In nothingness but try.

Envoi

Hail, Christel Engelbert, full of grace,
Jeanette Bonnier's astonishing niece!
Who sat by Jeanette's hospice bed,
Coming to the hospice day after day,
And vastness filled the small room
And the hilarious name Engelbert was a sky full of stars.

And a sky full of stars sat next to the bed
In broad daylight and many nights.
Rare beings like Christel Engelbert
Flow calmly like a candle flame.
Hour after hour Christel sat,
The night before Jeanette died, till Jeanette finally slept.

VERDANT VALLEY

The ringing telephone sobs to be picked up and when I do
It's someone I love but don't see anymore,
Calling from her car to ask
If I remember one of the beautiful places

In the world is
Verdant Valley in My Lady's Manor
In Maryland horse country which
We drove through together thirty years before

And she was driving through right now.
Mac Griswold, *you* were one of the most beautiful
Places in the world I ever saw and no doubt still are.
I picture you beautifully calling from your car.

Amalia Karabas, I am at a loss to surpass
The music of your name,
Itself a verdant valley to match your beauty.
The sound deserves a poem and will get one.

Caramba, Karabas! Imagine the joy and the blast—
The most beautiful woman in Queens
Is teaching her eighth-grade class!
Amalia is the curriculum! Karabas is the syllabus!

Seventy years ago, Raymond Sunderland, ten years old,
Emptied the school lunchroom with a foaming,
Thrashing, gnashing grand mal seizure and
Days later at home killed himself,

I don't know how, ten years old.
The thing he wanted most was attention
Which when he got it made him want to die,
St. Louis, 1946, Miss Rossman's School.

I pledge allegiance to the flag,
But Miss Rossman and Miss Schwaner rule
With a wooden pointer to thwack you with they never use.
Beautiful Mrs. Marshall has big breasts behind her blouse

And wears an FDR pince-nez.
Finally, I am old enough to walk to school,
Walking the back way through the tree-drenched private streets
To the concrete schoolyard where we play during recess.

Reading and 'riting and 'rithmetic
Toss and turn, yearn and burn.
We thrash and gnash—and explode with foam!
And need to go home.

I never knew Mrs. Marshall's first name was Pauline.
That didn't stop me from daydreaming about her even when
I was seated at my little desk right beneath her verdant valley
Standing there, who by now is dead, I suppose.

THE DROP DROOPS ACHINGLY BEFORE IT FALLS

Ninety percent of a man like me is mouth,
Exhorting on the page.
I find my seat on the plane
And get off in another place ready to.
It's not autobiography,
But it's not sentiment.
It's looking for the moon to take a ride to since Mars
Is too far and the moon is already in your bed
With you and in your head with you
Waiting to see what you will do.

Oh me oh my.
Absolutely everything is appallingly,
But I'm enthralled.
No one enjoys
The way I do the pause
In which I learn that I've been wrong.
I make me smile.
The sun breaks through the thunder beating its chest.
The dark sky breaks in two
And out pops spring goose-stepping.

POLICE CARS, AMBULANCES,
FIRE TRUCKS

Sirens are screaming, which means I'm still alive.
Sirens are singing, which means it's spring.
I keep my eyes on an approaching woman's chest
To see if there's hope and help. (There is.)
I glance there first and only afterward see a face
Bulging toward me out on the sidewalk.
I look forward to lust and life.
I look forward to the world's big breasts.
Sirens hurl warbling boxes down Broadway
Painted with the names of their hospitals.
Now and again there's a big red fire engine.
Here comes a hook-and-ladder
As crimson as Harvard, my alma mater.

What if police car, ambulance, fire truck
Arrive on the scene too late to save the republic?
Broadway is divided by a center strip
Of planted green, making on either side a speedway
For wobbling big breasts without a bra,
Or lesser breeds without the law.
The lovely opera student at Julliard singing *la, la, la, la,*
Does she want to go to Presbyterian Hospital on the west side

Or on the east side Weill Cornell?
You don't have much time to decide.
You don't have much time at all.
I remember the beautiful girl who died
When I was young and thrusting.

Is there such a thing as being *too* beautiful?
Can you be too beautiful to live?
Not in the moral sense of Christ, not of the spirit.
I'm talking about the physical, the vehicle.
Too gorgeous to believe
Is when you start to be a martyr
To your beauty and your beauty a disorder.
I look at you
When you're too gorgeous to believe
And I retreat.
I looked at her and wanted to stay and felt I had to flee.
She beat me to the door
And was no more.

Oh please! Don't start in on how bad.
Please. Let me sing that it's spring.
It doesn't ruin *everything* that the president is embarrassing.
Politics takes up a lot of space but
Actually I'm trying to think a long way back
To one of the bridesmaids, who was astoundingly beautiful—
But she did not like who she was.
She hated her movie-star legs and looks.
There was a look in her eyes

Of someone fighting off bad thoughts.
Years later, still young, when she committed suicide,
I remembered her look of lost.
I remember her suicide eyes, as if they were a white rhinoceros.

NOW

FOR ROBERT SILVERS

And you could say we've been living in clover
From Walt Whitman to Barack Obama.
Now a dictatorship of vicious spineless slimes
We the people voted in has taken over.
Once we'd abolished slavery, we lived in clover,
From sea to shining sea, even in terrible times.
It's over.

Look how the sunlight enters the bedroom and my dream.
Look how the radio alarm attacks me with an ax.
The plane I have to catch departs at eight from JFK.
Unbuckled and at cruising altitude, we'll excrete a white contrail.
I have to be there two hours before
We do. How beautiful the sky when you're below.
The Russian ambassador to Turkey was gunned down

Giving a friendship speech at an art gallery in Ankara
By a Turkish Islamic zealot
Pointing one finger upward and saying God is great.
Do not forget Aleppo! Do not forget Syria! he shouts,
Referring to the horror and the thousands wretchedly dead,
The little children, from Russian aerial bombing.
Russia is red and red the blood the ambassador bled.

The body on the floor
Is the late ambassa door.
You step over him to your study window holding a loaded gun
To your head and jump
Out to your death into the arms of Donald Trump.
Pigeons have painted the ledge outside the window white.
Now the day is over and it is time to say good night.

I hear the pillow hissing *auf Wiedersehen*.
I stumble out of bed and start sleepwalking.
WWW, White Western World, stand on your feet to greet, still asleep,
The arrival of the bride made of daylight all dressed in white.
Outbursts of pigeons explode white
As light in whorls of flight in the wonderful sunlight,
Then settle on cooing ledges and shit white.

I'm trumpeting the most dazzling imitation
Diamond ring you'll ever see,
Set by the expat genius jeweler JAR in Paris,
Whom nothing ostentatious can embarrass,
To celebrate the catastrophe of America, the American catastrophe.
The only possession of mine
God will want to grab

Is on my pinkie
When I'm laid out naked on the slab,
And here comes God—who's of course a she—
Who removes the ring,
And slides my corpse
For cremation
Into her big hot thing.

There was a very rich
Lady who lived on Liberty Island,
Who lied to herself and the world like Donald Trump.
Her druggy daughter, her only child,
Whose memory she liked to weep over and about whom she lied,
Had lived and died years before, and apparently the mother
Had behaved horribly when the daughter badly needed her.

The woman was arrogant.
People loved her.
Her life was luxurious. People like that.
There was an old
Woman who lived in a shoe.
Her fantasy was that she and her daughter
Had been fantastic together.

A person who smokes cigarettes these days,
Albeit only secretly,
A woman who smokes but hides it so no one sees,
And is careful about how she smells, no stink, no stain, no pain,
Now it begins to rain
In her lungs, these days when you're not permitted to smoke anywhere inside
A public place, even if she's elegant, is ashamed.

Give the poor bitch a break.
Be kind to poor inhuman us.
Aren't we all a bit like her and at least a little fake?
And wasn't America often quite generous?
In fact, my understanding is the Western heart is leaking pus
And the Western brain is near the end.
The Prophet Muhammad and his evil double have started to blend.

The president of the United States proclaims America First.
He doesn't know Mecca from Milan.
There's been a terrorist attack in Berlin.
Also, the leader of North Korea
Has ordered a new diet for border guards
That has given them diarrhea.
I repeatedly shot an innocent unarmed black man in the back who was fleeing

Into a park full of broad daylight. Good morning.
If you're a senior citizen, you won't really live long
Enough to know
The river of refugees has reversed its course,
Flowing the wrong way now on account of shock
And aftershocks and so many fools saying
Have a good day.

The United States of America, its ribs gauntly sticking out,
Tries to drink from a watering hole, all fifty states try,
Bulls mooing like cows, Gestapo everywhere,
But there's no water,
And this is not just in Flint, Michigan.
Girls and boys, a world you never knew is over.
I was writing a poem the other day that said so.

It said we've been living in clover
From Walt Whitman to Barack Obama.
Once we'd abolished slavery, we lived in clover
From sea to shining sea, even in terrible times.
Now a dictatorship of spineless vicious slimes
We the people voted into power has taken over
And it's over.

FOR SAYLOR, FOR USE LATER

The crocodile is eating the new barman!
There's a leg sticking out of its mouth.
Waiter, I'd like another one while I take in this gorgeous sunset.
Flavors of love and salt froth up on the pure white tablecloth of sand.
It must be fourteen feet long.
The hotel guests watch the leg ungrowing in chomps.
We're bringing you another drink on the house.

Then comes the moment when they say,
Actually, I really am going to die—
And don't believe it—
Do but don't—don't but *know*.
Some of their best friends won't,
Then one or two do.
They get their travel agent to fly them somewhere warm.

How much suffering are we expected to ignore?
Bring me more beach towels with my drink!
Waves drown and reappear and look the same.
TV solicitations for starving children and for caged dogs without hope,
Unloved, abandoned and abused, sedate
The row of coconut palms snoozing in deckchairs, tourists of grief
Enjoying the breakers exploding on the reef.

Everyone remembers Little Boy, the Hiroshima bomb,
And Fat Man at Nagasaki, but where are the hotel security guards
And guns, and for that matter what about a lifeguard?
Everybody remembers the time they saw a Lamborghini
Pink as a flamingo and heard the wonderful sound,
In the olden days of combustion engines, of noise power
Before the silence of electric.

A spaceship bigger than the world
Is coming in for a landing on the world.
What if an object larger than the world, more books
Than every library in the world, bigger than the asteroid
That will destroy the planet, more wingspan
Than every airplane in every air force put together ever had—
What if something really big is coming—and it's a girl?

ONE OF THE BRIDESMAIDS

I am remembering the unforgettable.
How the father of the bride
Took me aside
To say he knew I had vomited all over the chintz.

I hadn't—but desperately needed to escape
And took a borrowed car late at night out
On the dirt roads and silent highways of Westchester, drunk,
And got more and more utterly lost.

I had said to the best man, the groom's older brother,
That I would not be giving a toast, who said OK, perfectly all right,
And then called on me
To give the first toast.

My shocked toast was so brief
I sat down almost before I spoke.
There was an awkward tuxedo silence
While the room tried to figure out what had happened.

There I was in my drunken car
Looking for, somehow, *somewhere*—
Driving away from the wedding nightmare
Through the sweet night air.

I found a pay phone.
She said she would come and guide me back.
Who is this miracle arriving in her Corvette winged chariot—
And all of a sudden it's dawn!—softly saying: *Follow me, I'll lead the way?*

HYMN TO APHRODITE

Ποικιλόθρον᾽ α᾽θανάτ᾽ Αφρόδιτα

—SAPPHO, *Fragment 1*

I gather you were in the lobby
Minutes before.
Terrifying to almost see you again.
I smelled the shockwave, the burning air.

You were too sexual
To be bourgeois, screams from the jungle
On top of Mount Olympus.
You were too violently beautiful.

Last night I looked up at the sky,
Lights out as I was falling asleep.
There was the moon, a full moon, or nearly.
It was you.

I wasn't, but I could have been,
A god I was living in.
I chose not to come out
On stage and tell them what a poem is about.

Pubic hair that befits a goddess.
Pubic hair that equips a goddess.
That little arrowhead of pubic hair that
Magnifies your thighs' magnificence.

You look like a field of flowers.
You look like flowers in a vase.
You look like brains and breasts.
You act like life stabbing death to death.

I'm packing heat. That's a poem. My concealed
Carry permit is revealed.
I do what I do.
Peaches goes it alone.

I was like a god or
I was like the tiny hermit crab
Who walks around inside a borrowed empty shell
Bigger than he is for protection.

I carry the shell
I've borrowed like an umbrella
Wherever I go
Along the shore.

I dress up in one of my million-dollar suits.
I scuttle along Broadway,
Ready to be found out and eaten
Naked.

A thunderbolt from you
Walks through my front door
And knocks me to the floor
Where you and I, in love, still are

On top of Mount Olympus
Screaming your eternal estrus,
Eyes white and blank with blind
Ecstatic lack of sight.

PARIS, 1960

FOR NELSON ALDRICH

I was the Paris editor of *The Paris Review*
In a little office off the Champs-Elysées.
On the floor above our little room
Was Auto Europe, an outfit whose Anglo-American oddball salesmen,
Such as Digby Neave and Eddy Morgan,
Were wellborn fugitives hiding from a privileged life back home.

Unbeknownst to me, we were partly funded by the CIA
Through a CIA subsidiary with good Cold War intentions
Called the Congress for Cultural Freedom,
Itself funded secretly by the Kaplan Foundation.
If only I had known what was going on,
I would have asked the CIA man in Paris if I could join.

One fine day I was in the office doing nothing,
Or admiring the fabulous Larry Rivers cover for our next issue,
When God walked in and smiled
And said she'd like a job.
George Plimpton in New York had told her to introduce herself.
She explained she was the March Playmate for *Playboy*.

THE BLUE SUIT

Richard Anderson, master Savile Row tailor,
Opens the eleventh-floor hotel room door
Wearing a new suit so blue
It makes me smile,
Something no suit has been able to do for quite a while.
Welcome to room 1111 at the Carlyle.

When earlier in the morning Richard crossed the street
To the pharmacy opposite,
A stranger coming out of Zitomer's cried out,
"My God, that suit is *blue*!
Which was hilariously true.
All day long people remarked on it: the suit, and the blue, and the fit.

Richard and I walk around with, in our heads, a museum
Of, in his case, clothes he has made over the years,
And, in mine, clothes he has made for me that I have worn.
I have worn a lot of clothes since I was born.
Diapers eventually turned into bespoke
Suits that rise like ghosts out of the smoke.

Suits hang from their hangers in my mind
And faintly tinkle in the wind
Like wind chimes,
Prettifying my many crimes.
Mr. Hall at Huntsman was followed by his former pupil,
Now at his own firm, Richard Anderson at Richard Anderson.

What does a blue suit do?
What does a blue suit know?
It won't find friends in Moscow
When it's as electric blue as this one is.
It's a bit too Broadway musical, too Broadway show,
For Washington, D.C.

My dear severe Mr. Hall, whom I called the Reverend,
And who died a decade ago,
Wafts like mist through my mind
And falls like gently falling snow.
The wind chimes tinkle softly in the perfumed nights on Bali.
The trumpets of life-after-death blow.

SURF'S UP

Nothing to write home about.
No home to write home to.
Oh boohoo! I've never heard
Anything so disgustingly absurd.
The snow is falling crazily outside the window.

Now it's spring.
Still cold but the little birds this morning began to sing.
But the fucking pigeons are a constant curse.
Disgusting and absurd moans of human sexual intercourse
On the ledge outside my study window.

I'm leaping without wings,
Though I wouldn't mind having wings,
To you.
I'm leaping out my window to you.
Right through the screen of my computer into

Women don't like us anymore
And hold meeting after meeting over what to do.
Surf's up!
They ride the big wave.
They're not why the planet may be doomed.

Picture a scene right out of Disney Classics of giant saguaro cactuses,
Enormous nude green hairless tubes with arms
That look like prehistory reaching out without hands.
I hear the goddamned pigeons making a baby.
We share a desert.

What are you looking at?
I dug and dug to get out
A contact lens that it turned out wasn't in my eye
And got instead a ghoulish
Eyeball of blood.

It didn't hurt and I could see just fine,
Though it looked as if one eye was slowly cooking in red wine.
When I see your tits on FaceTime I see stars.
I see Stars and Stripes and Stars and Bars.
I'm in the finally-escaping-with-the-human-species-to-Mars

Mode, winged but without wings, coldcocked by love, out cold, surf's up.
Get into your Skype outfit.
Prepare for departure from this planet.
The last standing naked saguaros stand
There in the desert inside the Carlyle Hotel lobby.

I look in the men's room mirror at a man and his blood thinner.
Why, it's you, Eliquis, dear friend!
I see myself for a fleeting second looking like someone else.
I like the tiny Cartier watch the fellow's wearing.
I remember when he was once in Tahiti.

Lift me off the ground, mighty Ezra Pound!
Sing me your lyrical skunk spray of Cantos.
Robert Lowell, I will join you soon.
I remember DVF's enchantment apartment in the Rue de Seine.
I remember Mumbai when it was Bombay.

England—where the English are—
Used to smile with bad English teeth in the toxic coal-fires air.
It was the London of T. S. Eliot,
St. Louisan and expatriate,
Who found love late.

12/18